Intense!
Still feeling the effects!
— Kelly Dyer

GENIUS.
— Brownstone Poets

Stunningly profound!
Negative bliss.
— Halimah Ali Davis

QUITE GREAT!
— Shay Gaines

Quite marvelous!
— Michael T. Young

WORD.
— Redcat

YES!
— Brian Heffron

Great universal poem.
— Richard Ploetz

WOW! Get this one out for all to read.
— Mindy Matijasevic

TEN ... more

Also by John Jack Jackie *(Edward) Cooper*

TEN
New York, NY: Poets Wear Prada, 2012

WAX WOMEN, translator
Jean-Pierre Lemesle, photography by Henry Jacobs
Paris: International Art Office, 1985

TEN ... more

by John Jack *Jackie* (Edward) Cooper

Poets Wear Prada • Hoboken, New Jersey

TEN ... more

Poets Wear Prada
533 Bloomfield Street, Second Floor
Hoboken, New Jersey 07030
http://pwpbooks.blogspot.com

First North American Publication 2016
Second / Mass Market Paperback Edition 2016

ISBN-13: 978-0997981124
ISBN-10: 0997981121

Printed in America

Cover Design: Roxanne Hoffman

TEN ... more

For Brita and Lucian

Table of Contents

ROMEO AND JULIET, EXPLAINED

You cannot live for love.

Monday, February 11, 2013

VENUS AND MARS

Think of socks,
how difficult

it is to keep
a pair together.

Monday, April 13, 2015

EPILOGUE

How destitute
and slow

this present is:
like a clock missing

its minute hand —
love, second.

Tuesday, August, 20, 2013

TORUS II

Hearing Leonard Cohen touch
allows me to *re*-feel love

a continuous deformation,
topologically speaking;

only the hole remains.

Friday, March 22, 2013

TRUE IN LOVE

Do because you want —
no one must anything.

Wednesday, July 3, 2013

THE MASTERFUL VOICE

Love demands
the truth

of real
religion —

its implicit faith
that will not waver.

Tuesday, July 1, 2014

THE ADULTERER'S STIGMATA

Rug burns on elbows and knees

Sunday, September 18, 2016

A PURSUIT OF AMOUR
or The Hand of Face

Odd,
you know

longer
even look

like you . . .

Thursday, February 13, 2014

10

AT SEA

The trouble with loneliness
is fear of being alone —

and *whom*
you might meet.

Thursday, August 15, 2013

EMOTION SICKNESS

struck by desire
I fell at its mercy,
feeling none

Monday, June 10, 2013

12

WORDS FROM A STONE

Both terrible and vain
to have sought love

at a time one felt so little

Wednesday, March 6, 2013

SCHOLASTICISM

How many goodbyes
will fit in the head

before the end?

Sunday, May 10, 2015

TRANSIT OF VENUS

"Is she still as beautiful as she was?" he asked.

"Yes, but not when she's with me —"

Wednesday, February 13, 2013

15

SUMMER AND SMOKE

Summer makes me want to live —
 forever.

  Love did not.

Monday, July 15, 2013

SELF IN LOVE

Where have I been all my life?

Wednesday, June 15, 2013

❤ ❤ ❤

Acknowledgments

The author would like to thank Bob Heman for publishing "Transit of Venus" in *CLN WR* #50.

With the exception of "The Adulterer's Stigmata," all of these "aphorithms" have previously appeared on the author's blog, *These Are Aphorithms*, which can be found at http://aphorithms.blogspot.com/. The author explains *aphorithm* as "aphorism meets logarithm."

About the Author

JACK COOPER has read for Farrar, Straus, Giroux, served as research assistant for the Modern Language Association, was an ESL instructor for the ELESAIR Project, and is now Co-Publisher / Co-Editor at Poets Wear Prada. His American English translation of poems by Jean-Pierre Lemesle, *WAX WOMEN*, with photos by Henry Jacobs, was published November 1985 by International Art Office, Paris.

ABOUT THE TYPE

This book is set in Theano Didot, a free and OpenType typeface developed by Alexey Kryukov (b. 1974, Moscow, USSR) and released under the SIL Open Font License in 2007. A classicist and medievalist, Kryukov is a member of the History faculty at Moscow State University where he teaches Latin and Greek. Theano, her name borrowed by Krykov for his family of fonts based on classical texts, was priestess of Athena in Troy at the time of Helen. She and her husband, Antenor, a counselor to King Priam of Troy, advocated peace and for the return of Helen to Greece, and so were spared when the Greeks invaded.

The appearance of Didot — considered to be the first Modern typeface — coincides with the aftermath of the French Revolution. Developed in the eighteenth century by master typesetter Fermin Didot, the typeface was used by his brother, publisher Pierre Didot, for a highly prized 1818 edition of Voltaire's *La Henriade*. Once evocative of the Age of Enlightenment, modern renderings continue to flourish. Today, considered a monogram of luxury, Didot graces *Vogue* magazine.

Charles Fermin-Didot, a descendent of the Didot dynasty of Parisian printers and publishers, credits what he calls the "unprecedented strength and extraordinary power" of his ancestor's typography to the power of the French Revolution, posting these remarks at the Metropolitan Museum of Art's website:

> The harmony and openness of [Fermin Didot's] bowls exude generosity and freedom, the edges of his counters inspire "Égalité, Fraternité," and his hairline strokes have the sharpness of the guillotine. All in all, the contrasts are as clear as the revolutionary ideas: "Freedom — Equality, or you die."

www.ingramcontent.com/pod-product-compliance
Lightning Source LLC
Chambersburg PA
CBHW061759040426
42447CB00011B/2384